Seasons of Life

Avia Wideman

Presentation by *BookLeaf Publishing*

Web: www.bookleafpub.com

E-mail: info@bookleafpub.com

ISBN: 978-93-95890-76-2

First edition 2022

DEDICATION

I dedicate this book to my mom, she has lead the way for what it means to be hardworking and purse my dreams. My role model since day one, Thank you for believing in me mom.

ACKNOWLEDGEMENT

I want to thank my mentor, Tigelique Woods for bringing this dream of mine to life and for always pushing me to the best of my ability. My mom, for always supporting and believing in me with everything I do, she is my first love in life and has always been my shoulder. Lastly, my boyfriend who has supported me every step of the way in following my dreams.

PREFACE

Sea•son

/sēzen/

noun

plural noun: seasons

a proper or suitable time

Just like the weather, emotions are ever changing. There are rainy days, there a sunny days, windy days, and dark days, and it's okay to experience all of those.

Join me on my journey of going through the seasons of life.

It

It's consuming me.
Taking over my life, over my thoughts.
I have no say anymore.
I am the slave and it is my master
Breaking my back to please it,
Even if I'm losing everything.
I am confused.
Indecisive pleasures of
What do I do now,
Will this ever end
How do I fix this?
I am lost.
In an ocean,
No land, just water.
The toxicity resides on my tongue as it
surrounds me.
Sinking me deeper into the water,
It's drowning me.
And the only thing I see are the clouds and
boats,
Silently praying that someone will save me.
I'm scared.
As soon as I think this is my ending,
It spits me back up and pulls me to the surface.
Inhale.
Exhale.

I see the shore.
Land and water.
But as soon as I begin to breathe again,
It pulls me back under the water.
swallowing me whole,
my hand reaches for the surface hoping to stay
afloat but
Again.
I'm absorbed by the water,
Anchoring me down to the deep depths of the
unknown.
Planted.
Stuck in the reality of uncertainty.
Its ringing in my ears.
Make It stop.
It's controlling me.
Its eyes becoming my eyes.
Allowing me to see, but not experience.
 Changing me.
Turning me into a different person that even my
friends and family can't recognize.
It's calling me again.
Clouding my judgement.
The air is so thick,
I can barely breathe,
I can hardly see,
Blinded by the clouds of fantasy.
It is silent.

The only thing I can hear is the water ringing in
my ears.
Sinking deeper into the water,
The blood in my veins turning the color of the
ocean's face.
Lifeless.
It is a shark.
Circling me.
I am trapped with no way out.
Indecisive pleasures of
Will it help me?
Is It good?
Is It bad?
Is It a desire?
Or is It a hatred?
Is It anticipated?
Or is It unexpected?
Is It my savior?
Or is It my destroyer?
Will It ease my pain?
Or will It cause my distress?
What is It? It's me.

To Whom May Concern

To Whom It May Concern
It took me a long time to realize this, but I'm
angry with you.
Because you made me a Stereotype.
Ytou know, putting me in that Stereotypical
black girl without her father, box.
And I had no business being there
You stuck to the script society wrote for you,
And I'll admit , you played your part well.
You became everything they wanted you to be,
And because of that I had to be different.
Working hard, striving for A's in my honors
classes, pushing myself so I wouldn't be like the
rest of the girls on the sidelines that didn't have
their father.
I was determined to be different.
Because I didn't wanna become *that* girl.
Unlike you, I didn't want that -recycled script,
it's old.
But I get it, you were just playing the role
handed to you by your father.
So then I was force to play my role as the
daughter of the fatherless.
Forced to grow up too fast,

I watched other girls play hide and seek on the
playground,
While I played hide and seek with my emotions.
And if my emotions caught up to me,
Then Everything would come crashing down,
And I'd become what I fear the most.
The girl that makes excuses,
The girl thats weak,
That girl that is such an emotional wreck, so
afraid of abandonment
That she looks for love in all the wrong places.
I'm not her.
I can't be her.
I refuse to be *that* girl.
Did you ever think about what leaving me
without a father, would do?
Because I desired that male love that I never
recieved?
Do you enjoy how you made me like "them"?
A Stereotypical, fatherless black girl.
I needed you.
I need you to be my first love, not my first
heartbreak.
You were supposed to be there for me!
But yet your presence in my life was ever
changing like the weather seasons.
Playing with *my* life like it was double dutch.
Jumping in when you felt it was easy, and
jumping out when it got too hard.

Why couldn't you be different?
Why was I not enough?
You avoided *me* like you were playing tag,
Running away from me because you didn't want
to be "It",
Because that would mean that you would have
to chase me,
And face your responsibilities.
You wanted the role offered to you, because it
was easy.
 And Because you played the role offered to you
so well,
Society insisted I played the role they offered to
me.
But I refused to audition.
I refuse to give into the pressures.
And Because of that, I am strong.
And I guess, I have you to thank for that,
But don't be mistaken,
This is not a letter of gratitude.
You may have been for a necessity for my birth,
but not my existence.
You deserve no credit for who I am today,
So, To whom it may concern.
I am angry with you, but I still love you.
But not in the way a daughter should love her
father.
I love you the way someone loves an old friend.
A remembering feeling, but yet at a distance.

So yours respectfully,

Your not so average black stereotypical daughter.

The Letter pt. 2

The Letter

You planted a seed, but didn't even stick around
to water it and watch it grow.
Roots embedded in the same soil, stems
identical,
No one could ever deny that we came from the
same tree.
I was the petals,
And you were supposed to be the thorn to my
rose,
Harming only those who tried to steal my
blossom
But you rejected me like I was poison ivy,
Afraid that loving me would stunt your growth,
What was it that made you leave?
Was I too much to handle?
We share the same smile,
Same eyes,
A literal photocopy of your face,
You couldn't control how your life shifted when
I came along,
So you went for the alternative and deleted me
out of your life.
You rebooted your life without me.

Was it worth it?
You left a hole that only you could fill.
But I kept trying.
I just wanted you to be the daddy that I
deserved.
You were supposed to show me what the winner
of my heart looked like,
But instead you showed me what the last place
looked like.
Here I am, a full grown flower,
I grew my own thorns, developed my own,
with the help of my sun, of course.
I have blossomed and bloomed with no help for
you.
I'll continue to shine on my owns,
but my thorns won't ever disappear,
that's the mark you left.
I'm left with scars that I don't know how to heal.
All I ever wanted was to be watered by your
love
So tell me, will you ever love me again?

Sweet

Sweet

Eight Years Old.
Sound of cars beeping,
Visuals of street lights,
Buses stopping,
All of it infecting my body.
Watching with little brown eyes as factories
turned into little brown houses.
And the loud pace of city life transitioned to the
quiet pace of suburbia-
My Grandparent house.
The cold tiles rubbing against my bare feet,
My grandfathers chocolate eyes staring down at
me,
As I poured the sweet strawberry syrup into the
dull white milk,
Always adding a little extra strawberry.
I lived in a utopian society where my life was
sugar-coated and tasty,
Always leaving me craving more.
Why did I want to grow up so fast?

Eighteen years old.
The sound of the wind howling,

The sensation of chills crawling up my body,
The whispers of the darkness,
I'm numb.
Home.
Alone.
With nothing but a cold glass of white milk on
my nightstand.
Now I prefer the dullness to the sweetness.
Something I once shared with my grandfather, is
no longer enjoyable.
He moved beyond the clouds and nothing was
ever the same.
I watched my grandfather deteriorate in front of
my eyes,
I wasn't even allowed to shed a tear.
I was told to be strong.
A little girl who forced herself to put on a mask
to save her family.
But why didn't I save myself?

Eight years old.
The melodic sound from the white postered
truck,
 With its symbol of attraction.

My little brown hands reaching for the purchase
of satisfaction.
The sweet sticky sensation of ice cream running
down my skin.
All my problems could be fixed with a wet
towel, wiping away what clung to me.
The only thing messy about my life were my
hands.
Why didn't I save myself, or even grasp I could?

Eighteen years old and I don't know where to
go.
I'M SCARED.
Carouseling through revolving doors of
expectation and responsibility.
Loading the gun to play the everlasting game of
russian roulette with possibilities,
That are uncertain to me.
No longer care free,
But instead stuck,
Cornered into the reality of uncertainty.
Is this where I want to be?

I see a mirror image of myself, gasping for air
My brain trying to comprehend
Racing heart beats, scrambled thoughts
Memories.
Goals.
Dreams.

Trying to piece together and finish the puzzle of
my life.
Will I ever connect the pieces that make the full
picture?

Why did I think I could handle this journey?
Chains of now adulthood threatening me,
Barriers of responsibilities try to lock me up.
Obligations calling, reaching me through my
phone
With indecisive tones that ask questions,
That only my eight year old self can answer
How much syrup do I have to add to get back to
the sweet?

Untitled

It's been 1,195 days since I gave my last lover
the key to my heart and
locked myself out

Opened doors for him, broke down barriers

Too bare to see through the blinds while blind to
the storm

The rain was gone, I couldn't see clearly .
Allowed him to explore every inch of every
corridor

Unbeknownst to me, too caught in the falsity of
a fantasy
There's a lot of fallacies in the measure of a man

I Authorized fabricated infatuation to take
residence
When in fact he couldn't rize to the authored
standards he fabricated
no longer a tenet in my own home,
he was the landlord

I was praying to my god yet I had no place to
landlord

Revolving doors kept turning,
Surrounded by obscure windows
Contemplating suicide while he kept watch

Happily ever afters played out in front of me
On repeat
Thought I was the lady of his life but turned out
to be just another lady in his life

Conversing with satin in the dark
 when I should have been reading genesis

Desensitized to tracks in our living room
Cuz he always forgot to come up out his forces
 before he forced his way into this fortress

Our house was never home
A shaky knob on a screen door
jiggling with the slightest turn

Ignoring the knocks
Cause opening my door twice was unimaginable
But you,

A glimpse of hope peeping through the peephole
Picking my lock, forcing your entry,

Breaking my windows

Turning his vandalism into a magnificent
masterpiece
Using your pencil to erase the pain of my past
Taking my stained glass and its scattered pieces
to make a marvellous mosaic

paint this destructive nightmare
into a lucid dream

1000 words hidden in the canvas
you took this abandoned one story and made
into villa of perfect poetry
a beautiful motif you are, poetry in motion

A juxtaposition of despise
adjust your position to be
A literary depiction of light

Absolving all Affliction
An alliteration abiding in my life
You are constant in a poem, I hope I never finish

365

It's been 3153600 seconds, 525600 minutes,
8760 hours, 365 day, 52 weeks, 12 months, 1
year since I fell in love.

3153600 seconds since
you became mine,
I,
I Knew you belonged to me,
Indefinitely, and even that,
didn't seem long enough for me.

525600 minutes
when I am with you,
world stops.
and time?
Fails to exist in our world.

8760 hours.
My soulmate, you showed me how to love.
Something to be embraced and not feared.
Erased a philophobia & welcomed warmth of
love.
something that was foreign to me.

365 days

my heart beats,
for you and is fueled by,
the blood of our love.

52 weeks
life is unloveable without you.
without us

12 months
you
are my

1 year
everything.

Heartbreak Anniversary

I miss him.
Everyday I think about him, how I loved him so passively, gave him my entire heart without ever asking for it in return.
Learning to let him go was probably the hardest thing I've ever had to learn.
The most painful experience to date was the day I knew that I lost him.
It's funny how I saw it coming and still the pain seemed so unbearable.
To loose someone who I wanted to be in my life forever was unfathomable,
my mind drifting to wonder…
Why did that happen to us?
Were we right for each other, but the timing was wrong?
Or were we just lessons to be learned in each others life?
I don't know but I do know that this pain will last until I find my next subject of obsession. I still love him.
Yes.
I know that I'm wrong for it.
But I can't help it.
I invited him into my world,

let him take the key to my heart.
Unlock something that I thought would stay
locked forever.
He left his footprint on me as he proceeded to
walk all over me.

I guess I should thank him, he forever changed
my outlook on life, on relationships and on how
I treat myself.
Sure I put on a strong face but he broke me and
forced me to rebuild myself up.
The toxicity of his self absorbed love poisoned
my stem, damaged my growth.
Both he and I watched as my leaves fell to the
ground and eventually, my roots became
infected with his virulent enchantment.

I had to plant a new seed, a seed of self love.
His inadequacy to cherish the admiration I had
for him was a blessing hidden behind the
misfortune.
I then took the time to learn myself, and
everyday I fall more in love with myself.
 There are days where I think that I am incapable
of love but I know that I am.
Someday, when God knows Im ready for him,
I'll be blessed with an amazing husband who
will know how to love me the way I need to be
loved. I miss my ex but I can't keep giving him

this power over me. Besides deep down I know he is only a scapgoat for my father. I am learning to be content with loving myself and being the only one that loves me. Things still hurt but its okay because I know that I will get through it. Troubles don't last always, and when its my time to shine, my sun will be bright.

Sorry

Sorry

Baby I'm sorry,
you continue to tell me time after time.
But i opened my eyes to realize that all of that
was just lies. you destroyed me.

Baby I love you,
you Constantly disrespected my feelings like
they were just toys you could play with when
you were bored. and you call that love?

Baby please,
My eyes are dried up from the tears that you
caused. There's no more chances, all the pennies
I threw in your fountain wishing that one day
you'd act right but before you could I ran out of
pennies.

Baby don't go,
My mind and my heart at war, can't decide if
you deserve another countless chance. My mind
wants to be your executioner, while my heart
wants to declare you not guilty.

Baby, I didn't mean it.
Tears racing down my face my eyes drowning in
the red sea. My heart sank into my chest, chains
weighing me down, sinking me deeper with each
of the convincing lies you tell. My heart, cut off
by the lack of oxygen, lacks the ability to make
the rational decision so my mind steps in.

Baby, I'm sorry.
I proceeded to tell you this time.
I finally opened my eyes to realize that this time
would be the last.
You destroyed my heart but I'm ready to pick up
the broken pieces and glue myself back together.

Baby, I love you.
But I love myself more. Crazy part is you told
me you loved me but you didn't even stay to
help pick up the broken pieces and clean up the
mess that you made.
Baby I'm leaving.
I got comfortable in this uncomfortable season,
but it's time I picked a season. I decided to give
myself a chance, ready to throw countless
amount of pennies in the fountain wishing for
my success.

Baby I'm gone.
Exiting the game, quitting the control you had
over my heart. Ready to pick a new character
and start over.

And Baby, I mean that.

One Last Kiss

One Last Kiss

Can I have one last kiss?
I didn't know that the last would be our last.
so can we make this one count?

you pull me towards your body,
your soft lips brushes against mine,
In the moment of the last melodic tune that our
lips would echo,

nothing else matters, but me and you.
I stare deeply into your chocolate orbs wishing
that I could keep this moment frozen in time.

I'm not ready to pull away, to never be able to
sing the duet uttered by the rhythm of our lips, to
know that someone else will have access to you
the way I did.

Can I have one more hug?

My arms wrapped around your neck as you
bring yours to my waist, nothing but my chest
against yours.

our heartbeats joined together in perfect
harmony.
Didn't want us to separate,
knowing the minute we did the vibrations would
stop.

I'd be left with the void of agony, a heart split
into two so
Can you tell me you love me one more time?

Let the words drip from your lips
the sweetness of it sticking to my memory,

so I know that this wasn't all in my head.
So that I know you never wanted to hurt me.

Give me one more reason to believe that we
weren't a mistake.
That this tune was pure and intentional.

I keep hoping that there's hope for us.
waiting for you to reach out to me,
Tell me your sorry, that you didn't mean it.

So we could erase the pain and write a new
story.

My head laying against your chest,
 laughter echoing in your ear.
Bring that back.

On my knees praying to god that this was just an
interlude.
But I open my eyes, there's no repeat button for
this song

You left me.
you hurt me so badly,
that you left me clingy to the blessing of a
broken heart

just so I wouldn't forget us.

But it's over
and there isn't a one last time.
The memories still reside

 i can still hear the noise of a smile,
the musk of confidence
and the sweetened sugary savoriness of your
luscious lips

The pains still there,

no more us.
just me.

just you.
And I wish you all the best,
I'm not sorry for loving you,

I'm not sorry for you loving me.
But, if we meet again,
can i have.....one last.....kiss?

You

You
The oxygen that runs through my lungs,
the blood that travels to my heart to keep it
beating.
You are everything I have ever needed,
I spent nights closing my eyes tight wishing for
mr, right,someone to excite me and,here you are.
A breathe of fresh air,
meeting you was like a flower absorbing water.
Rehabilitation.
You saved me from myself.
Loved me better than I could ever imagine from
anyone.
Freshwater after all the salt water.
I can breathe again.
Knowing that you love me,
The air in my lungs is fresh, vibrant, renewed.
You were healthy, the toxicity was gone.
Baby you, are my everything.
Losing you would literally leave me lifeless on
the side of an abandoned road,
you are the thing that gives me life.
the king to my queen on my chessboard,
Checkmate
I finally met my match.

The game was finally over for me.
You are the love of my life, when I look into
your eyes, the galaxies stop.
Never knew a love like this could exist for me.
A love that runs deeper than the 71 percent of
water on this earth.
This poem is the ocean, bottomless, endless,
So many things I can say, but not enough words
to accurately capture your love.
So many things I could say about you,
Your chocolate orbs, I get lost in every time.
The way they glisten when the sun shines on
them,
The way they make me feel warm on the inside
when I stare into them,
The corners of my mouth are always curved
uspide.
The reason for that:
You.

Timeline

Timeline
The first week.
All the veins and arteries robbed of an organ, because you hit the stop button on us. My airway cut of, drowning in the tears that seemed everlasting.

Month #1
Every little thing reminds me of you. Moments go by and I can still feel your presence. Still feel your skin against mine like it was yesterday. Keep trying to replay where we went wrong, how did we end up here. No contact like we never knew each other. how was this so easy for you?

Month #2
I try to convince myself that what we had wasn't real love. That just maybe if I convince myself that we weren't real, that the idea of us never existed than maybe this wouldn't hurt as much. That my heart is broken, that I'm okay without you.

Month #3

 I miss you. I embrace the idea of what we once were, and begging to God in the dark in the four small corners of the brick walls that just maybe you'd come back. That I dreamt this all, and the phone would ring and I could hear your velvet voice through the phone and everything would go back to normal.

Month #4
Try to destroy the memories of you in my mind because I know we weren't ever gonna last, and there's no hope for us, but i can't. Being in a place where you once were, your aroma lingers in the air, I keep replaying the moments we spent together. Vivid images of you popping in my head at random moments.

Month #5
Movies and TV shows remind me of the time we spent together, wishing that I can rewind us and start from the beginning and press play. Fix where we went wrong, the roughness of your hands still fresh in my memory, The cloying of your lips on mine. Why haven't you gone away yet?

Then I realize the timeline of our love can't be erased, so I should stop trying. It's ceased, but my timeline will continue, without you, I hope

one day that the pain won't accompany the
memories, that we will remember our timeline
as something beautiful and insightful, because
that's what it was: to me.

See Me

A lost soul,
Drowning in a pool of her sorrows
Desperately waiting for a lifebelt, something to
keep her above water.
She keeps swimming, her little feet flipping in
the cold water,
Trying to avoid all the dangers the sea brings.
But the sharks were desperate for blood,
And there she was, sitting in the middle of the
ocean,
Sharkbait.
Mommy couldn't save her, too busy worrying
about other lost souls,
Daddy wanted nothing to do with her.
God didn't see or hear her desperate calls for
help.
Her lungs filled, airway cut off.
Her souls fighting to preserve.
All she wanted was to be see.
She desperately needs to be see.
Can anyone see?
Please.
See Me.

Fairytale Love

Fairytale Love

I didn't think that love was possible for me.
I didn't know that I could become a princess
until I met you.
I never imagined the glass slipper fitting my
foot,
Lost at sea, with no home
But suddenly I became part of your world,
It was unfathomable that you could return my
voice to my body.
To see the beauty in all of my ugly,
To give me a life that is beyond three wishes,
To open my eyes to see all the colors of the
wind,
I didn't have to try to make a man out of you,
You catered to my dreams,
and together we built this unbreakable tower of
love.
No matter how far I go,
Our coronation of love will never be outlawed.
Life would be very cold without you, I would
never ever let you go.
I was almost there, never knew there were
puzzle pieces missing.

The best thing I never knew I needed,
One kiss was all that I needed, after many
poisonous apples, to be awaken in a spirit of
love.
Never again will my finger be pricked by the
thorns,
because i found my prince.
I found my fairytale love.

Scrambled Love Thoughts

why can't i hate you? why can't i let go of you?
I'm tethered to you, constantly trying to cut ties
to you like red, but i can't rid myself of you,
you're stained on me like red. your hold on me
as solid as sement. I find myself wishing i could
hate you as deep as the sement but I can't.
desperately chasing your feelings like the way
we chase leaves in the fall. Wanting to tie you
down but can't because like the leaves, your
feelings were light and blowing away from me
as the wind gets heavier and i'm stuck in
between seasons, frozen like winter & rainy like
spring, blistering like summer, and lukewarm
like fall, constantly feeling like we're gonna fall
off. I got comfortable in this uncomfortable
season we're in. I want to let go, but i want to
hold you close., hoping that this love drug is
strong enough to restore the deadly virus we call
a relationship. but as i look into your eyes i
realize that i was just there for you to utilize,
You are the drug that heals me and kills me all at
the same time but i don't wanna stop usin, why
am i letting you infect me? You were my
lifesaver and now you're my killer. Did you

enjoying watching me decay? How could you
pull the plug and leave me flatline?

Dear Me

Dear me,
Now the one thing I would tell you, is to love yourself.
Oh and to not rush growing up.
Cause Life is a game that was destined to make you lose.
But you find cheat codes and keep playing and that's how you win.
The world is your opponent, it's goal is to make you loose.
There are many times where you'll wanna quit,
But you don't.
Simply just press restart.
Learning to love yourself is the start.
That'll save you so much time and energy.
I let other people create my character, and make me the sim they wanted , instead of creating myself as a character I wanted to be.
Controlling me,
Pushing X to make all the people I care about exit my life, all for people who didn't even care about my well being.
Life pushed my buttons so hard, making me want to quit life.
But I didn't.

I pressed pause,
rewinded the game
and started to love myself.
So with each twist and turns and trials and
terrors,
never loose sight of the end game.
The prize is you.
Cause baby once you love yourself,
Life can't beat you.
So Me,
Hold on to life a little longer,
don't give up.
Because the end of the game is rewarding.
Sincerely,
the girl whose still trying to find the cheat codes
to life.

Daddy Issues

I'm so sick of love songs, so sick of people
doing me wrong, I'm so sick of all things that
belong to love.
Cause what did love ever do for me?
You see Daddy left the hive, when i was five,
and i was derived of a first love.
I'm just young bee trying to survive.
But since he left, I can't seem to get things right.
Constantly trying to fill the void to avoid these
daddy issues.
Along came a boy, that temporarily gave me a
fix.
But i failed to realize that i was just there for
him to utilize
he was a lame tryna to play games I wasn't
summer walker, All I ever wanted was for you to
say my name,
but you shady, ain't tryna beg you to be my
baby.
I guess this wasn't destiny,
And I became the child of a broken heart.
The same things kept happening,
It was a cycle.
Their art was my pain,

Don't understand what they had to gain,
It's a shame I could've been something.
Daddy I'm so sick of letting people use me
because you bruised me due to your inability to
love me.
Your lack of love cause these absence of my self
love.
Daddy I'm so sick of all these daddy issues.
So sick of the rambling questions and thoughts.
why wasn't I enough?
why did you leave me?
daddy why wasn't I, alone enough for you to
stay?
I sacrificed my self worth hoping one day I'd be
worth your love again.
Daddy what's wrong with me?
Why does everyone keep leaving?
Daddy I'm so sick.
Daddy, I just wanted you to love me.

#BLM

#BlackLivesMatter

It's 2020, but y'all vision ain't clear.
Racism still exist.
It's not gone.
Mirroring exactly what our ancestors went
through.
55 years later and the civil rights movement isn't
over.
Same Story, Different names.
Emmit Till translated into Tamir Rice

My people are dying, each and everyday
fighting for freedom for a chance to live,
for a chance to be heard
You use your thumbs to tweet that hashtag out
because another black man was killed.
For you the hashtag is just a hashtag. A way to
show that you're an ally, to show to the world
that you're this activist. But for me? It's more
than a hashtag. #BlackLivesMatter isn't a
trending topic for me, it's my reality. Everyday I
never know how my days gonna end. If i'm
gonna be lying down in my queen size bed or a
hospital bed fighting for my life,. You can

participate in the protest, sign petitions, but let me ask you this, When BLM isn't trending anymore and all of this dies down, will you still be for us?

This is For

This is for..

This is for Trayvon Martin, the boy who just
wanted to eat his skittles and chug his arizona.
This is for Sandra Bland, the women who was
just trying to smoke her cigarette.
This is for Oscar Grant, a man tryna get home to
his baby girl
This is for Tamir Rice, the boy who was trying
to be a kid playing cops and robbers.
This is for Mike Brown, the boy who never got
to go to college.
This is for Laquan Mcdonald's. The 17 year old
boy whose life was taken away too soon.
This is for Breonna Taylor. The women who
never woke up in her own home.
This is for all my black brothers and sisters who
were robbed of living because of the color of
their skin.
This is for the the future black boys and black
girls.
This fight we are fighting, is for them.
Their Black Lives Mattered. Your Black life
Matters. My black life matters.